One Stroke Design

By Dale Swant

THIRD PRINTING

Published By:
©1993 SCOTT PUBLICATIONS
30595 EIGHT MILE
LIVONIA, MI 48152-1798
ISBN# 0-916809-68-4

No. 3483-12-93   PRINTED IN U.S.A.

Introduction

Most of us have admired the many beautiful flowers, birds and butterflies painted on plates and vases at ceramic shows. These pieces are lovely, but look complicated and seem beyond our ability. Most ceramists never attempt these projects because the feel a lack of artistry. While artistic talent is an asset to all projects we undertake in ceramics, it is not a necessity. Ability to create beautiful pieces is similar to other challenges in life...learning what tools to use, how to use them and a lot of practice.

No one rolls a perfect 300 game the first time he bowls, neither will he be able to create a blue ribbon piece finished in one-strokes on our first attempt. It can be learned, however.

This book is an introduction to the proper use of one-strokes along with helpful hints to make your creations easier to accomplish. In addition to mini-projects as we go along, included are several complete techniques (including the techniques for the two pieces on the cover) for you to try.

We think you will find one-strokes easier to use than you thought, and a lot of fun.

Dale Swant

Table of Contents

What is One-Stroke?...4
When to Use One-Strokes..4
Do I Use One-Stroke on Greenware or Bisque?.................................4
Choosing Between Underglaze and One-Strokes.................................4
How Do I Know What Colors I Have?..5
What Tools Do I Need?..5
What Brushes Do I Use?...5
What Effects Can I Achieve With One-Strokes?.................................6
How to Care for Brushes..6
How to Prepare Your Colors...7
How to Mix Colors..7
How to Change Colors...7
How to Load Your Brush...8
How to Hold Your Brush...9
How Much Color Should I Lay Down?..9
Outlining for Fine Lines With One-Stroke....................................10
Shading With the Same Color of One-Stroke...................................10
Shading With More Than One Color of One-Stroke..............................11
Using Brush Pressure to Your Advantage......................................11
Sponge Work With One-Stroke...12
Stencils and One-Strokes..13
Drybrushing With One-Stroke...13
Creating a Wash With One-Stroke...14
Spattering With One-Stroke..14
The Airbrush and One-Stroke...15
Banding Wheel Decoration with One-Stroke....................................15
China Painting with One-Strokes...16
The Majolica Technique in One-Stroke..16
How to Use Mask With One-Stroke...17
Wax Resist and One-Strokes..17
One-Stroke Over Transparent Glaze...17
One-Stroke Under Transparent Glaze..18
One-Stroke Over Matte Glazes..18
One-Stroke Under Matte Glazes...19
Embossing Glaze and One-Stroke..19
One-Stroke Over Froth...20
One-Stroke Over Underglaze..20
One-Stroke and Crackle Glaze..21
Adding One-Stroke to Color Ceramic Slip.....................................21
One-Strokes for Lettering or Printing.......................................21
One-Stroke and Lace...21
One-Strokes and Porcelain...22
One-Stroke Defects..23
Summary...24
Glossary of Terms...25

ONE-STROKE TECHNIQUES

Potato Block Printing on Ceramics......*By Dale Swant*.........................27
Pinecones on Porcelain..............*By Sande Scoredos*........................31
Magnolia and Hibiscus...............*By David Hoff*............................33
Pretty Pansies......................*By Diane Murphree*........................35
Classic Vase........................*By Natalie Kahn*..........................37
Polychrome Effect in One-Stroke......*By Leila Sloan*.........................38
Frostina, The Snow Woman............*By Larry Rhodes*..........................40

1. WHAT IS ONE-STROKE?

One-stroke is a member of the underglaze family of ceramic colors. This family includes opaques, which are a combination of clay and color pigment and require three coats for solid coverage. One-strokes are concentrated color pigment with no clay added, and may be translucent or opaque. These colors are used to create and copy attractive designs and ideas on ceramics.

Similar to grammar school watercolors, one-strokes are the base for washes, outlines and small areas of concentrated color. All are soluable in water.

Although fired one-stroke colors are similar to those of opaque (three coat) underglazes, each has completely different properties and uses. A good way to keep the two straight is to remember, "underglazes" as we will call them in this book, require three coats for solid coverage and are opaque. Opaque and translucent underglazes not intended for solid coverage are called "one-strokes."

Being opaque means no light can pass through. Translucent properties mean light will pass through but in the process, be diffused. Therefore, translucent one-strokes will allow colors under them to show through. Opaque one-strokes will cover any colors underneath.

2. WHEN TO USE ONE-STROKES

Every ceramist should learn when and how to use one-strokes, since they present the opportunity to accomplish techniques not possible with other ceramic media.

Although we can create many of the same shading techniques with stain as with one-strokes, a look at the end use of the piece will decide which is needed.

Any ceramic piece designed for utility, such as coffee cups, ashtrays, dinnerware, etc. must be glazed. Since most glazes are not suited to detail design work your design must be put on "under the glaze" in the form of solid underglaze coverage or detailed one-stroke work.

Stained projects are beautiful and easy to do, but they are for decoration only. Any piece that will be exposed to heat or to water must be finished in glazes, and if you want a design on the piece it must be put on with one-strokes or underglazes.

3. DO I USE ONE-STROKE ON GREENWARE OR BISQUE?

It is a matter of personal preference. It is safest to use one-strokes on bisque pieces to avoid breaking a fragile piece of greenware after spending many hours of work on it. Firing your piece ahead of time prevents careless breakage, but does cost an extra firing.

Both bisque and greenware projects turn out nicely, and since you soon learn the "feel" of handling greenware, most ceramists undertake projects on greenware. The additional advantage is that painting on greenware allows a greater range of combination of techniques. We will be covering some of these later in the book.

4. CHOOSING BETWEEN UNDERGLAZE AND ONE-STROKES

When making a choice as to which paint to use in your design work, it is necessary to make a choice between opaque (three coat) underglaze or concentrated, opaque or translucent underglazes, "one-strokes."

Since both are used in a variety of combinations quite often, the easiest way to keep the two apart is to remember that underglazes are for wide area coverage while one-strokes are used for small detailed areas.

One-strokes are not for large area coverage due to the impossibility of painting them on wide areas without streaking. Remember, one-strokes are always poor choices for background coverages because they are concentrated, detail colors, although you do have some opportunities to employ them using airbrushes or in sponge techniques. Each will be outlined later.

5. HOW DO I KNOW WHAT COLORS I HAVE?

If this is your first experienced with one-strokes and you have only the knowledge of glazes and stains to go on, you will recall the color in the glaze jar is seldom the finished color. The final color is not achieved until the chemicals in the glaze react to the firing temperatures in the kiln.

When using stains, the color in the jar is the finished color. Stains do not have to be fired and no chemical reaction has to take place so the true colors are in the jar.

The same holds true for one-strokes..."What you see is what you get!" This is important since you need not refer back and forth to a color chart as you go along.

If you do not have the proper color on hand, you do have the ability to mix them to the desired shade. You can be confident that your finished piece will fire to the color on your palette, because you are mixing pure color.

If you should decide to mix a one-stroke with a three coat opaque underglaze you will again be dependent on the firing to bring out the true color, as your three coat opaque underglaze contains clay and must have a glaze cover to show the full color.

You may mix one of your pure one-stroke colors and they will fire true.

6. WHAT TOOLS DO I NEED?

Obviously you will need a variety of brushes for your work in one-stroke. A complete breakdown of recommended brushes and their care follows.

In addition to brushes you will find a use for a silk sponge, a lambswool sponge and a sgraffito tool. It is also handy to have a divided palette or tray for mixing and diluting colors, a bowl for water to clean brushes, and a spatula or palette knife to use in mixing colors.

A wise investment is a turntable to place your piece on while working. A turntable allows you to rotate your piece as you go, avoiding the risk of breakage from too much hand pressure.

It is always recommended that you purchase the finest quality tools and materials from the very beginning. You get what you pay for and the ease of using one-strokes or any other medium is greatly enhanced with good tools even if they are more expensive.

7. WHAT BRUSHES DO I USE?

The type of brushes you need most likely will be recommended by your instructor to start with, but there is a basic assortment we can suggest. Others may be added as the need arises.

To start with, a selection of three red sable liners is needed. (Illustration A). A number 1 or 2 liner will be used for fine pointing for features, lining, striping, spotting, dotting and other fine detail work.

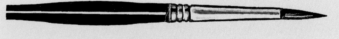

Illustration B
Red Sable Round Pointed Brush for Shading Effects

The last category common for one-stroke work are the square red sable shaders (Illustration C). These brushes enable you to create many shading effects and also may be used for drybrushing techniques. Common sizes are 4, 6, and 10.

Illustration A
Pure Red Sable Liner for Fine Line and Detail Work

A number 4 liner is used for detail work also, but the finest details should not be attempted with this brush. It works best for filling in solid areas of color.

Your number 6 liner will be used for the largest areas of detail work.

Next you will need one or two pointed round brushes to be used for shading, drybrushing and varying strokes. (Illustration B).

Illustration C
Red Sable Shader Used for a Variety of Shading Strokes

You will also need a glaze brush, which you probably already have.

The quality of the brush you purchase will often determine the ease of painting. Dollar for dollar, the more expensive brushes are your best buy and will be easier to work with in the long run.

8. WHAT EFFECTS CAN I ACHIEVE WITH ONE-STROKES?

The possibilities are almost limitless. One-strokes are ideal for shading, airbrushing, fine detail shading, shadows, watercolor techniques, china painting, blending and special dimensional effects.

Each of these subjects will be covered in detail as we go along.

9. HOW TO CARE FOR BRUSHES

Taking good care of brushes will increase their life for years. A quality brush, properly cared for seldom wears out. You may loose a few hairs over a period of time but proper care will prevent most of this from happening.

Most important to remember about taking care of brushes is to keep them clean. The best policy is to have a dish of water beside your working area. Clean your brushes the minute you are finished with a color. Since one-strokes are water soluable, this is easy.

When swishing brushes around in water, do not push bristles against the bottom of container to work out color. This is a sure way to cut off bristles. Bristles of brushes are held by a metal ferrule. Putting excess pressure on bristles will bend them back over this ferrule. (Illustration D.)

Although the end of the ferrule is not razor sharp, bending bristles while cleaning will cut or wear them off if you do it very often.

Swirl brushes around in the water above the bottom of the container in a beating motion. If they do not come as clean as you wish, run them under the faucet. You may also wash brushes in a mild detergent as long as you wash out the detergent when done.

After each brush is cleaned and while they are still damp, form bristles into a point for pointed brushes, flatten bristles to a razor edge for flat brushes. **Never** leave your brushes bristle down in water, even if you are going to use them again in a few minutes. This is a sure way to break down their natural ability to maintain body.

Illustration D
DO NOT PRESS BRISTLES AGAINST BOTTOM

Care also applies in storage of brushes. There are several means of storing brushes. If you do not have a commercially made holder, standing them on end with their bristles up, in a jar will work fine. If yo do not plan on using them for a long time, they should be stored in a flat box such as a cigar or shoe box. To keep the bristles in shape for a long period of time, add an agent such as glycerin to your water. After cleaning and shaping, brush bristles will dry fairly stiff, keeping their shape until you are ready to use them again.

These tips on care of brushes apply to all brushes, not just those you will be using for one-stroke work. Most tips are just common sense. A good rule of thumb is if you are in doubt, don't do it!

10. HOW TO PREPARE YOUR COLORS

You will find this a simple step. As previously mentioned, one-stroke is concentrated color pigment so it should not be used straight out of the jar. It should be thinned with water.

With your palette knife, transfer a small bit of color from its jar to your glazed tile, divided dish, etc. for mixing. (Illustration E). Add a few drops of water. Be sure to add only a few drops at a time. For most work you want to thin your one-stroke to a creamy consistency.

This consistency will give you true solid color of the medium. The more water you add to the thinner, the lighter the color will become.

If you plan on using only a few brush strokes of a certain color, you may mix and dilute your colors using a wet brush. If you use this method, however, you want to be sure that you only need a few strokes. This combination of water and color will be impossible to duplicate exactly if you need more of this color later.

To be sure the color is what you want, always test it. After completing your mixture, stroke it a

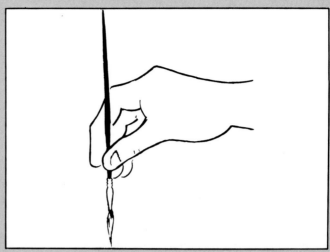

Illustration E
MIX COLORS IN DIVIDED DISH OR ON PALETTE

few times on a piece of white paper or sample bisque to check for color. If it is too dark, you may add a little water or if not dark enough add more color from the bottle.

You will find that darker colors will need more thinning than lighter.

11. HOW TO MIX COLORS

The beauty of using one-strokes is their flexibility to make colors you want. As mentioned in Section 10, you can control the intensity of the same color simply by the amount of water you mix with one-stroke straight out of the jar. The more water you add the lighter the tone. This addition of water will give you the widest range of color tones using the same basic color.

However, this method will only give you the range of hues within the same color base. For example, you can make a lighter red, or what appears to be pink, by starting with red one-stroke and adding water.

You cannot change the base color from Christmas Red, for example, to a blood red simply by adding water. This must be accomplished by mixing base colors together.

Naturally you have to mix one color into another and the choice of which goes into which will make it a little easier.

If you want to make a darker color lighter it is

best to put the darker color on your palette first and mix the lighter into it a bit at a time until you get what you want.

If you are trying to darken a color, start with the lighter color on your palette and mix in a darker color.

By using this method it gives you a little better control. Use a small amount of color at a time, as adding two colors together can change the end combination rapidly.

Also, if you use too much and have to keep adding color to change the original, you could end up with way too much for your project. However, you can save this excess in a small, air tight jar for future use.

It is best to mix colors before adding water. If your one-strokes are quite thick you may need a few drops of water to make mixing easier, but add water to bring your new color to painting consistency after you have mixed the right color combination.

12. HOW TO CHANGE COLORS

Any one color manufacturer does not offer the full range of color possibilities. If you purchased every different color from all ceramic one-stroke companies you still would not have all the possibilities. Therefore, you will at one time or another want a color you do not have.

This may be accomplished simply by mixing several colors on hand to create another. Although most one-stroke products are similar in manufacture, it is not a good idea to mix brands. If there are any differences, they will show up on

Continued on page 8

your finished piece. Most ceramists use a particular brand for certain types of paints, so it probably will not be a problem.

As we mentioned earlier, you can think of one-strokes as being very similar to watercolors and mixing of two colors in one-stroke is almost indentical to that of mixing watercolors. It is just that simple.

First, you want to recall that you cannot create the primary colors of red, blue and yellow through mixing. These have to be purchased as your base colors. In theory, as we learned in grade school, you are able to make every color in the spectrum from these three basic colors.

However, the process of knowing how much of each to use, to make a full rainbow does take experimentation and time which most of us don't have.

This is why we usually begin by purchasing many ready-made colors at our ceramic dealer and changing only a few if we do not have the color we need.

To change any color to a lighter tone, we simply add white one-stroke to it. We can make a dark color lighter by adding a lighter tone of the same color to it. (Example: Combine a Dark Green with a Light Green to make a Medium Green.)

A light color can be made darker by adding a darker color in the same tone. (Example: Baby Blue can be made darker by adding Royal Blue to it.)

To create completely new colors, use your primary colors. Red and Blue make Purple. Red and Yellow make Orange. Yellow and Blue make Green.

Different proportions of each color within these combinations will determine the hue of the final color. These newly created colors are called secondary colors.

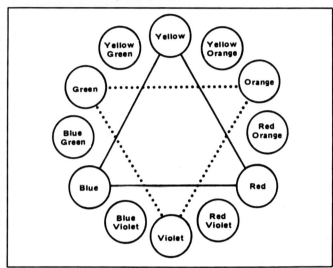

Illustration F
COLOR WHEEL FOR COMBINATIONS

A good way to determine what color you will get by mixing two colors together, before you try mixing, is to follow the color wheel shown here. (Illustration F).

By mixing in this manner you will come as close to the color as possible.

No matter how good you become at mixing colors, it is still experimenting, and you should try the color on a piece of paper or sample chip of bisque to be sure it is right.

13. HOW TO LOAD YOUR BRUSH

The first rule to remember is never dip a dry brush into one-stroke colors. First dip brushes into water, and squeeze out the excess, leaving your brush moist. Brush loading techniques to achieve certain effects will follow in the next section. There are general brush instructions, however, that apply to all techniques.

To load your brush properly, first think how the color acts when it is on the brush. Brushes are similar to fountain pens. The tip of the brush does all the work while the body of the brush holds the reserve. As you work, the color will flow from the body to the tip of the brush.

Load your liner by immersing the bristles entirely in your mixed color. Pull the brush through the color, turning the brush at the same time, so your bristles form a fine point. Do not put too much pressure on the brush when doing this or you will squeeze out all the color.

Do not stroke your brush against the side of the mixing palette either. This is a habit many of us have. This procedure will also squeeze color out of your brush.

To load your square shader, follow the same basic procedure. After you have loaded the color in the bristles, press both sides of the tip of the brush flat. This will form a nice sharp edge.

14. HOW TO HOLD YOUR BRUSH

Even if you have loaded your brush properly, you can still make errors by holding your brush the wrong way. To achieve the correct brush strokes in one-stroke work, learning the effects of pressure on the brush bristles has a lot to do with the end result.

If we could all be as comfortable using a brush as we are holding a pencil, we would have a great advantage. Often times this is the reason for troubles we encounter in using a brush for lettering and fine detail work.

You should not try to hold your brush in the same manner as you do a pencil. What we want to accomplish in brush work is a free flowing stroke. If you try to to hold your brush in the same position as you hold a pencil, you will end up working with the flat side of the brush, rather than the tip.

Properly, you should try to hold your brush as straight up and down as you can. This position is not comfortable to most of us, so a little practice is a good idea. (Illustration G).

Load your brush with color or water and practice strokes on a piece of paper. After you have done this for a while you will get used to it.

Illustration G
HOLD BRUSH STRAIGHT UP AND DOWN

While experimenting, apply different pressure to your brush tip to learn the effects different pressures will have.

The more pressure you exert, the fatter the lines will be and the more color you will lay down.

15. HOW MUCH COLOR SHOULD I LAY DOWN?

As mentioned, the amount of pressure helps to determine color depth. If you find colors look too light after your piece has been fired, you have not applied enough color. If you put too much color on a piece using one-stroke, there is a possibility of the color popping off after firing.

Areas where this danger is greatest is in detailed areas of your piece. As with any paint, one-stroke tends to build up in crevices if applied too heavily.

The proper application is accomplished, as the name indicates, by stroking the color on. Do not apply one-stroke by flowing it on like glaze.

Simply load your brush properly and apply it in smooth, even strokes.

Since we have the advantage of seeing the actual color as it will appear after firing, you can always go over your color if it is dark enough.

One thing to remember! All of your brush strokes will show when applying one-stroke. Even, smooth coverage is important. This is much easier accomplished with one-strokes than it sounds since you are working in small areas only. If some of your strokes do streak you can go back over and smooth them out.

16. OUTLINING OR FINE LINES WITH ONE-STROKE

For this technique you will want to use your darkest colors. Black, dark brown, dark greens and dark blue are all good colors. Black will fit in with most every color combination.

If you have a piece that has a background color you may want to outline using a complimentary color. (Example: Dark blue outlines on a baby blue background.)

When preparing these colors for use, do not thin them too much. Since they are outlines, you want the color to be as deep as possible. Add only enough water to paint them in as an easy, smooth stroke. This type of work is done with a number 1 or 2 liner brush.

Load the brush with color, filling it to it's capacity, twirl the brush as you pull it out of the color, to form a fine point. (Illustration H).

Remember, this brush acts like a fountain pen, allowing the color to flow down the brush body to the tip as you work. Hold your brush as straight up and down as you can, using light pressure as you move along your lines. The heavier the pressure the thicker and darker the line.

Illustration H
Outlining or Fine Lines with One-Strokes

17. SHADING WITH THE SAME COLOR OF ONE-STROKE

By using a combination of water and one-stroke on your brush, you can paint shaded areas in one-stroke, from light to dark.

For this type of work you generally use a square shader brush. Mix your color in the proper manner on a tile or palette. Now, load your brush with water and remove the excess. As discussed earlier, all brushes should be damp or contain slightly more water.

Load the corner or about one-quarter of the brush with color. Practice a stroke on a piece of paper to test your finished stroke. The finished stroke will look like the one picture here. (Illustration I).

Your brush must be loaded with water to allow the color to blend with the bristles but not overly damp to make the one-stroke work through the hairs of the brush to the other side. If this should happen you will end up with a solid line of color instead of a shaded effect.

A very important point to remember is to always clean your brush between uses of this stroke. You will be able to use several strokes from one loaded brush, but as you proceed, colors in the heavily loaded corner will work into the unloaded bristles, eliminating your shaded effects. Rinse your brush often.

If the finished stroke looks streaked it means you did not have enough water in your brush. If this should happen, load your brush again with water and color.

Illustration I
SHADING WITH SAME COLOR OF ONE-STROKE

The pressure you exert on the bristles should be against the loaded side of the brush. Be sure to practice these strokes before attempting to use them on a piece. If done properly, these strokes will blend your color from a very light to very dark. The brush should be moved in an even, flowing stroke. Do not stop in mid-stroke or it will show.

18. SHADING WITH MORE THAN ONE COLOR OF ONE-STROKE

You may build depth in your shading strokes by laying different colors over each other. This is done by stroking the darkest color on the bottom and applying a lighter color over the top.

You can accomplish a similar effect, much easier, by applying two colors on the same brush. (Illustration J).

First, load your brush with water, stroke out the excess until brush is just moist. Now, load your brush with your first, usually lightest, color. Now, tip the corner of the brush into your second, or darker color. Apply this doubly-loaded brush combination in the same manner as outlined in the previous section. The result will be a shaded blend of two colors.

In this technique do not try to stretch the number of strokes you get from a loaded brush. Two colors will mix rapidly as you stroke. It is important to clean your brush after several strokes and load again.

It is possible to load your brush with a three color combination. (Example: Load with medium green, tip one corner with light green and the second corner with dark brown.) This

Illustration J
Shading With More Than One
Color of One-Stroke

combination will give you full range shading for leaves, petals, etc.

19. USING BRUSH PRESSURE TO YOUR ADVANTAGE

So far we have noted that care should be taken in the amount of pressure placed on brush tips. This holds true when you want to outline or in shading effects.

Since the pressure is a variable thing, it is best to learn how to control it and make it work to your advantage. A round, pointed sable brush is most favorable for this technique, although it is possible to use your liner.

Load your water-dampened brush with color in a twirling action, to form a fine point. Start your stroke on the tip of the bristles. As you move your brush, press down the bristles, making your color application heavier. (Illustration K).

Gradually raise your brush again to its tip. The amount of pressure in mid-stroke, determines the width and the amount of color applied. For best results, this stroke must be done quickly. When using this stroke, always work from the center of the subject out.

This is ideal for creating long, thin leaves, bamboo or other effects. Each stroke is a leaf with this stroke. The size and width of the leaves are determined by the amount of pressure you apply. If you cannot get the leaf as wide as you want simply change to a larger brush.

Illustration K
Using Brush Pressure for Design Work

When using this stroke you can also take advantage of shading techniques. You may either build up several shades of color or tip your brush in another color as outlined in Section 18.

20. SPONGE WORK WITH ONE-STROKE

The effects you can achieve with a sponge using one-stroke are commonly used in background work although you may complete some fill-in work. Most commonly used is a silk sponge although there are a variety of others that may also be used to create patterns.

Start by putting out a small amount of color on a tile. Immerse your sponge in water and wring out the excess until it is damp. Wet your sponge in a small amount of color. Pounce the sponge on a piece of paper or practice piece of bisque. This evens the surface blob of color and works it into the sponge allowing you to apply it in a uniform manner. you may now pat your piece with color. (Illustration L.)

For an even greater variety you may apply several background colors by using different colors of one-stroke on top or around each other. Your designs are applied over this background once it has dried.

You may also create varied effects by loading your sponge in the same manner but instead of pouncing or patting on the color, drag the sponge across your piece to produce a streak effect. Best results in application are achieved when you do not apply too much pressure.

If you have a turntable your sponge may also be used to produce swirls and circular designs. Center the area of the piece to be painted in the center of the turntable. Load your sponge in the same manner, being sure to pat on separate piece of paper to even colors. Rotate your turntable, holding the sponge steady in one spot. This will produce your swirl or circular pattern.

Sponging is commonly used as a base for outline work. Sponge a circle with orange-pink one-stroke keeping the heavy color coverage to one side. Go back over it with your detail brush loaded in dark one-stroke to create a piece of fruit. Leaves are added for detail. (Illustration M).

Illustration L
Sponge Work With One-Stroke

Illustration M
Peach-Fine Line And Sponge Work

21. STENCILS AND ONE-STROKES

There are a number of ready-made stencils on the market or you can make your own by cutting a pattern from stencil paper purchased at your local ceramic studio. It is advisable to work with a piece of bisque fired to cone 06 when undertaking stencil work. Main reason for this is the amount of pressure you will exert on the piece while holding the stencil in place.

With your stencil in hand place it in position on your piece and hold it firmly so it will not move while you work. (Illustration N). Although both a brush and sponge may be used in this technique, a sponge does give you more control over your project. Simply load your sponge as discussed in Section 20 and pat on your color.

When applying color do not pat too much color at one time along the stencil edges. An outline will result if you do. If you want the outline, fine, however a soft, but solid coverage of color is usually desired. It is better to put on several coats of color until you have the coverage desired. If you want a soft center color with darker edges this may be accomplished by the amount and number of coats you apply in a given area of the stencil. You may then follow up by adding details in the stenciled areas.

Illustration N
Stenciling with One-Stroke

22. DRYBRUSHING WITH ONE-STROKE

This method of using one-stroke is ideal to fill in and accent work in ceramic projects. It is accomplished using most brushes but is probably most effective using shaders or dry rounds. Moisten your brush as usual and load with color. This time when loading, however, you will want to press out your color more than usual to make your brush drier in color. When applying color in this method press lightly so that the hairs of the brush separate as individually as possibly allowing color to go on your piece in thin lines. (Illustration O.) A test is important on paper or sample piece of bisque. The trick is loading the brush properly.

Illustration O
Drybrushing with One-Stroke

23. CREATING A WASH WITH ONE-STROKES

The primary use of a wash in one-stroke work is for antiquing effects on detailed pieces. Making a wash solution of one-stroke is as simple as any other preparation of one-stroke, which is the combination of water and color.

A proportion of 3 to 4 parts water to one part one-stroke is effective. Again, it is best to test this to determine if it is the color you want. If it is too dark, simply add more water. If it is too light add more color, a few drops at a time. Mix an adequate amount. It is always wise to mix more than you think you will use. It is almost impossible to match if you run short.

Wash is best applied to bisque, since you will be handling your piece quite a bit and may have a tendency to hold it too tightly for greenware to withstand. Also, there is the danger that you will remove detail when sponging the wash off.

To apply washes, use your large brushes. Dip in water and squeeze so brush is moist. Apply your mixture to the entire piece and let dry. Now, dampen your sponge and wipe down piece, leaving color in the crevices, removing it from raised areas. If you should happen to remove too much wash, which is easy to do, simply apply another coat of your mixture, let dry and wipe down again.

Wipe down until the effect is pleasing to you and fire to cone 06. Apply the proper number of coats of transparent glaze and refire.

You will undoubtedly encounter ceramists in a hurry, who try to short cut the process by

Creating a Wash with One-Strokes

eliminating the extra firing. Applying glaze over a wash without firing the piece first is risky.

They may be lucky and get this to work, but eventually the short cut will ruin a piece. Since both glaze and one-strokes are water soluable, applying glaze over unfired one-stroke can't help but loosen and mix the two.

The end result would be a fuzzy or runny antique. DON'T DO IT!!!

24. SPATTERING WITH ONE-STROKE

This technique is accomplished using a stiff brush. There are special spatter brushes available at your ceramic studio for this purpose or an old tooth brush will serve the purpose.

Procedure is to mix your color as normal, load your brush, being sure that the color is well within the bristles so that it will not drip. Bend the bristles back with your finger over your piece and then let go. The color will spatter all over your piece forming an excellent dot pattern background for other work. You may repeat the process as often as you wish for desired coverage. The size of spattered dots are controlled by how you thin your one-stroke. The less water you add the smaller the dots; the more water or the thinner your mixture the larger they will be on your piece.

Spattering with One-Stroke

25. THE AIRBRUSH AND ONE-STROKE

One-Stroke is an ideal medium for use in airbrushes. As you know, airbrushes create a fine mist of color. Applied with our concentrated colors, it is very effective. Any airbrush that is recommended for ceramic work will function perfectly. Simply thin your one-strokes with water to a 50-50 consistency. If you want a lighter color simply add more water. Control of the color is in the application. The lighter the application the lighter the color. The greater the number of applications the darker the color. (Illustration P.)

There are many uses for one-strokes using an airbrush. This procedure will produce excellent backgrounds for other one-stroke work. Airbrushes give you the ability to build several different colors over each other for background variety.

It is imperative that you clean your airbrush thoroughly after each use and also between color changes even if they are immediate. Cleanse with water. Spray clear water through the nozzle to be sure it is clean too.

An airbrush is effective with the stencil techniques. Simply hold stencil in place, spray on color, then go over with your fine line work.

Illustration P
Airbrush with One-Stroke

It may also be sprayed over certain glazes for added color effects. (We will discuss one-strokes in combination with glazes shortly.)

26. BANDING WHEEL DECORATION WITH ONE-STROKE

Techniques with one-strokes are possible by using both motor and hand driven banding wheels. Pieces chosen for this technique should be round or circular. It is impossible to decorate a square piece on a wheel without knocking it off.

Pieces painted in this manner are usually given a background color first. Backgrounds may be of opaque underglaze or one-stroke sponged or airbrushed. Once background is applied and dry, place piece on wheel and secure.

Banding your piece may be accomplished with a variety of brushes or sponges. Since you load brushes with a limited quantity of color at one time you may wish to use a sponge. Squeeze your sponge tightly and place in one-stroke mixture. When pressure on the sponge is released it will absorb as much as color as possible. Again your mixture of color and water will determine the degree of color on your finished piece.

Start your banding wheel in motion and hold your sponge at an angle to your piece, from top down, at 45 degrees. This angle applies if you are using a brush too. The amount of color and the width of your bands are determined by the amount of pressure placed on the brush or

Banding With One-Strokes

sponge used. It is also possible to obtain multi-colored bands by loading your brush or sponge in one color and tipping it with another before applying. It is difficult to apply one color over another in separate applications since you run the risk of the second color wiping off the first.

27. CHINA PAINTING WITH ONE-STROKES

To accomplish the many china painting techniques use square shaders or china painting brushes. This technique is a matter of mastering brush strokes and knowing what your colors will do. You may use the china painter's finger painting techniques also. As in normal china painting techniques, work is done on glazed ceramic or china pieces. The same principles apply as in normal china painting. As with anything, practice makes perfect but you can accomplish similar results. Colors are built the same and fired into the glaze. An additional coat of spray glaze may be added and refired.

The beauty of this china painting procedure is that if you make a mistake you may simply wipe it off with a damp sponge and start over. This enables you to get all the practice you want and never ruin a piece.

China Painting With One-Strokes

28. THE MAJOLICA TECHNIQUE IN ONE-STROKE

Although most often undertaken on larger pieces such as bowls, pitchers, frames and plates it is possible on smaller pieces.

To begin you must clean and fire your piece to 06 bisque. Next, spray or dip-glaze your piece in an opaque or matte glaze. If you can apply this type of glaze smoothly with a brush it will work. It must be applied smoothly, however, since this type of glaze moves very little when fired and a brush will not be as smooth as when sprayed or dipped. Transparent glazes can be used in this technique but since they move more in firing they may not be as effective.

After glaze has dried place piece in a working position on a turntable. Working on a turntable is recommended since it is easy to rub glaze off with fingers.

When you have applied a pattern to your glazed piece use a large brush and apply one-stroke in generous floating strokes. The brighter colors are most effective. When completed simply fire piece and you will have a finished Majolica-like piece.

Majolica Technique

29. HOW TO USE MASK WITH ONE-STROKE

Most ceramic color manufacturers have a masking material to use in connection with both underglazes and one-strokes. Their use prevents any of your background color from overlapping design areas. They are in liquid form.

To use simply outline pattern on greenware piece and fill in with mask. Apply wherever design will be painted later. After mask is dry you may spray, spatter, sponge or brush on background colors. You do not have to fear lapping into design areas because mask will repel paint. Colors may be wiped off or left to dry without worry.

After background colors are dry simply peel off the mask by starting it with the point of a sharp tool. Use a rubbing-rolling pressure with your finger tips to take it off. The area under the mask will be clear for design or detail work.

You may not want to paint masked off areas. It is effective to fire, glaze and refire the piece too.

Mask with One-Stroke

30. WAX RESIST AND ONE-STROKES

Another product used for masking is wax-resist. It is used in the same manner as outlined above but rather than peeling it off it is fired off.

This product is used many times by giving your entire piece a background color then painting on the mask to a design area. After dry, color is applied over the entire piece again. When the piece is fired the wax resist fires off leaving the first background color showing through the area where the wax resist was painted. Glaze and refire.

31. ONE-STROKE OVER TRANSPARENT GLAZE

The combination of one-stroke techniques over a transparent glaze is quite common and the results are fine. In this technique apply three coats of transparent glaze to a bisque piece. Since this is the surface you will work on, place piece on a turntable so you will not have to handle it too much. Next, trace on design. Load brush well with one-strokes for this type of work and use floating strokes. When piece is fired to the proper cone the two mediums join and produce a fine finish.

Over Transparent Glaze

32. ONE-STROKE UNDER TRANSPARENT GLAZE

Although techniques are possible when using one-stroke over transparent glazes, unless they are the kind that move a little when fired your fancy designs will not look as you thought they should. Due to this, it is advisable to take care with transparents. After the designs are applied to greenware, fire piece to 06. Three coats of transparent glazes are applied, then fired again to 05-06. This category of glazes are transparent so one-stroke designs will be visible through the glaze.

Use of transparent glazes over one-stroke is not limited to clear glazes. It is possible to obtain effective pieces using pastel shaded transparent glazes. Even some of the more brilliantly colored transparent glazes produce excellent results. (Example: Try a black one-stroke design under red transparent glaze. You will have a lively oriental style piece.)

Under Transparent Glaze

33. ONE-STROKE OVER MATTE GLAZES

Matte glazes have the property of moving very little when fired. Effective techniques over this glaze are possible. To do this simply clean and fire your piece to 06 bisque. Paint on three coats of matte glaze. Remember this type of glaze moves very little when fired so it is important to apply in even coats for a smooth, final product. After glaze is dry, simply apply one-stroke design over glaze and fire. One-stroke designs may also be applied effectively over colored matte glazes.

One-Stroke Over Matte Glaze

34. ONE-STROKE UNDER MATTE GLAZES

Since matte glazes usually produce a soft colored finish the majority of colors are classified as opaque. There are a few translucent pastel colors that may allow color to show through. Design possibilities under the glaze are limited. A clear or transparent matte glaze is commonly used over one-stroke work. Simply paint design on greenware along with any desired background. Fire to 05-06. Again, remember to take care to apply matte glazes smoothly to avoid brush marks.

One-Stroke Under Matte Glaze

35. EMBOSSING GLAZE AND ONE-STROKE

Marketed under a number of brand names such as Brocade, Emboseese, Flair, etc., properties of these products are basically the same. They are used to create embossed or raised surface effects on ceramic pieces of greenware or bisque.

There are several methods of using one-stroke in combination with embossing glaze. First, place the embossing material on palette with your one-stroke. These are placed on palette separately. Thin one-stroke to creamy consistency. Load brush with embossing glaze and tip in one-stroke color. The procedure is effective when creating raised flower petal designs.

Proceed on greenware first by tracing on a flower and leaf design. Using one-stroke, paint leaves and stems. Following the above procedure, load brush with white embossing glaze and tip in desired color of one-stroke. Work from top of pattern down and from inside of flowers out. You may make flower centers a different color with the same procedure. Fire the piece to 06. Paint with clear glaze, being sure that it does not pile up next to the embossed areas and refire. There is no need to glaze over embossing glaze.

Although embossing glazes are manufactured in different colors you may tint white to make other shades by mixing with one-stroke. Use the most brilliant or dark colors. Pastels would not be strong enough to tint the product to your satisfaction.

Embossing Glaze and One-Stroke

36. ONE-STROKE OVER FROTH

Again, marketed under a variety of names, this glaze is used to create frothy, snow-like texture on pieces. Your experience with this media may only have been to create special effects such as snow on Christmas pieces. It does have other uses, one of these is in combination with one-stroke.

To accomplish this project begin by sponging the glaze on the outside of a greenware piece. Three coats are necessary for desired coverage to create a froth finish. After dry, trace on pattern and paint details with one-stroke. Fire piece to cone 06. This will give you a foamy appearance piece with a design on it.

If you use this technique on the outside of a vase or similar piece it will be necessary to paint the inside with glaze and refire. Do not glaze over your finished design.

This product is manufactured in colors which you may paint over. Again, if you want to change the color of froth you may do so by mixing froth with undiluted one-stroke colors. The bright, strong colors are best.

One-Stroke over Froth

37. ONE-STROKE OVER UNDERGLAZE

In the beginning of this discussion we pointed out that although one-strokes are underglazes they are concentrated while opaque underglazes are the same color pigments with clay added.

The two are used together regularly with the opaque colors serving as a background and design work done in one-stroke over them.

A one-stroke wash may also be used to antique details on a piece that has been colored with underglazes.

After pieces have been completed they are fired to 06. Then they are glazed and refired to 05-06.

One-Stroke over Underglaze

38. ONE-STROKE AND CRACKLE GLAZE

One-stroke may be used under clear or transparent crackle glazes very effectively.

Simply paint the design on your piece of greenware as normal and fire to cone 04-05. Then apply proper number of coats of clear or transparent crackle and refire to 05-06.

After the piece has set a week or so after being fired, make a wash of black one-stroke and water. Apply this mixture to the outside of your glazed piece with a brush. Work the wash into the cracks. Let dry and wipe excess off.

You will find that this is a very pretty piece and looks like an authentic antique.

One-Stroke and Crackle Glaze

39. ADDING ONE-STROKES TO COLORED CERAMIC SLIP

One-strokes are excellent coloring agents for ceramic slip. After all, underglazes are simply clay in combination with one-stroke color pigment. The need for colored ceramic slip does not come up too often, but it is handy to know that it is available. It would be expensive to attempt a large amount of this on a regular basis. This is best experimented on small pieces.

One use for colored slip is in double casting as is often done with colored porcelain. This is accomplished by pouring one color of slip into a mold such as a bowl. Let this set-up to half its normal thickness, drain mold and immediately pour in another color of slip. Let this set-up for the other half of your bowl thickness. You may decorate this or simply fire and then apply glazes inside and out and refire.

This same thing may be done with colored glazes for almost the same effects.

40. ONE-STROKES FOR LETTERING OR PRINTING

If you ever want to print your name or names of persons on projects, one-strokes are used on the pieces to be glazed. Although black is most commonly used the other darker colors work as well.

Since one-strokes are concentrated, they have many of the same properties as printer's ink. It is possible to make your own rubber stamps of names and designs. We use our one-strokes like stamp pad ink and apply to pieces with these rubber stamps. Colors are thinned slightly for this use.

You may also use other objects as stamps. Unusual shapes will work fine. Most of these unusual shapes such as cog wheels are of metal and will not hold color very well, making application uneven. Try it. You will enjoy the results.

41. ONE-STROKE AND LACE

If you like to lace drape dolls or use lace as trims, one-strokes wil come in handy. There is no need to drape your piece only in white lace. By adding one-stroke color to white slip you may produce fine pastel colored lace. All that is necessary is to add a few drops of one-stroke to a two ounce jar of slip. The darker colors should be used sparingly, while the pastel shades will require more color to effectively tint slip. This slip tinting property is not limited to ceramic slip. One-stokes have high-fire properties and may be used to tint porcelain slip as well. Some one-stroke colors do not break down when high-fired so a color should be tested before a piece is started.

42. ONE-STROKES AND PORCELAIN

A high-fire (cone 6) clay body such as porcelain does not limit one-strokes. You may use the same detail painting techniques on porcelain greenware as well. When fired to maturity the porcelain vitrifies fusing one-strokes into the clay body. One-stroke colors do not require additional coats of glaze in this use. When one-strokes are fired on porcelain the end result is a more satin-like finish which is much brighter than the colors on ceramic bisque. Not all colors fire true at high temperatures and should be tested as previously noted.

We do advise when using one-strokes on porcelain not to work on porcelain greenware. We suggest that you fire your greenware to cone 019 before beginning a project. Do not attempt to clean until fired either. At this low temperature, the clay body is soft enough to be cleaned and pourous enough to absorb one-stroke colors.

An additional use for one-stroke is in the coloration of porcelain slip. As mentioned in the previous section color pigment is strong enough to be high-fired in most colors, by adding color to porcelain in small amounts. This should not be attempted on any large pieces since the true translucent colors of porcelain are better cast from chemically formulated porcelain slip.

One-Stroke Painted on Porcelain

ONE-STROKE DEFECTS

As with any ceramic media there are times when pieces do not turn out the way they were planned. This section includes some of the problems you may encounter when using one-strokes, their cause and how to correct or repair them if possible.

DEFECT: One-stroke curled or peeled away from the surface over a matte glaze after fired.
CAUSE: Applying too heavy a coat of color.
SOLUTION: Avoid this in the first place by loading brush properly. It is difficult to correct such an error but may be attempted by china painting techniques or by using an overglaze such as gold to cover these areas.

DEFECT: Crazed or cracked glaze over one-stroke.
CAUSE: Underfiring bisque or cooling too rapidly.
SOLUTION: Refire at one cone hotter.

DEFECT: Pinholes in glaze over one-stroke work.
CAUSE: Underfiring, glazing over a dusty piece or firing too rapidly.
SOLUTION: Use the same glaze, fill in holes and refire.

DEFECT: Cloudy clear glaze over project.
CAUSE: Underfiring.
SOLUTION: Refire at proper heating rate and cone.

DEFECT: Shiny matte or smooth textured glazes.
CAUSE: Overfiring.
SOLUTION: Fire properly in the first place. This type of error cannot be corrected.

DEFECT: Grainy clear glaze over piece.
CAUSE: Not a heavy enough application of glaze.
SOLUTION: Warm piece in oven slightly and reapply another coat of glaze and refire.

DEFECT: Shivering or separation of color from piece.
CAUSE: Incompatable clay body and color which occurs during expansion and contraction.
SOLUTION: Nothing can really be done to repair piece but the knowledge of what colors may cause this will help to avoid its happening.

DEFECT: A streaked, blotched finish of an opaque underglaze background.
CAUSE: Not loading brush properly will cause this or not applying the proper number of coats.
SOLUTION: If discovered on bisque reapply another coat and refire. If found after glaze firing nothing can be done.

DEFECT: Faint one-stroke colors after bisque firing.
CAUSE: Thinning colors too much with water or too thin an application of color.
SOLUTION: Reapply color to desired tone and refire.

DEFECT: One-strokes peeling away from bisque.
CAUSE: Too heavy an application. Happens in depressed areas in antiquing techniques.
SOLUTION: Reapply color to areas after scraping off loose paint and refire.

DEFECT: Streaked or running strokes under glazes.
CAUSE: May be caused by attempting to glaze over unfired one-stroke.
SOLUTION: Do not do it. Cannot be repaired.

DEFECT: Too dark one-stroke color after fired.
CAUSE: Too heavy an application.
SOLUTION: Some color may be sanded off the bisque with grit paper.

DEFECT: Plugged airbrush.
CAUSE: Not thinning solution of water and one-stroke enough or may be caused by not cleaning airbrush well enough.
SOLUTION: Clean airbrush. Remix one-stroke and water to a thinner consistency.

DEFECT: Colors too dark.
CAUSE: Not thinning one-stroke with enough water.
SOLUTION: Mix and test colors on paper or sample bisque piece.

SUMMARY

To total up all the points we have covered in a short outline is difficult in a small space. The following, however, is an attempt to condense each section of this book down to a one sentence synopsis. If you need more information about a particular phase of one-stroke work as outlined here simply refer to the number at the beginning of each sentence and turn back to that same numbered section in the body of the book for the full details.

Don't be afraid to try new ideas and when you do be sure to put in some practice. Whether it is a new brush stroke or just a new idea, one-stroke work is like most things in life, 10% talent and 90% hard work.

1. One-strokes may be both translucent and opaque "underglazes".
2. Use one-strokes on design pieces to be glazed.
3. Use one-strokes on bisque and greenware.
4. Use opaque underglazes for wide area coverage, one-strokes for design and small area coverage.
5. Colors in the jar are the finished colors.
6. You need primarily brushes and sponges for one-stroke work.
7. Liners, shaders and round brushes are primarily used in one-stroke work.
8. Many effects are possible with one-strokes.
9. Always clean brushes properly. Care of tools is most important.
10. One-strokes are thinned with water.
11. New tones from the same base color is possible.
12. Different color shades may be mixed to create new colors.
13. First step in loading a brush is to moisten it.
14. Hold your brush as straight up and down as possible.
15. Pressure on brush determines amount of color applied.
16. Outlines are created using tips of liner brushes.
17. Shading with one color of one-stroke is possible.
18. You may shade with more than one color of one-stroke on the same brush.
19. Use pressure on brush for special effects.
20. Sponging one-strokes is used to create backgrounds.
21. Use stencils and apply one-strokes with a sponge.
22. Loading brush lightly will allow drybrushing.
23. A wash of one-stroke and water is used for antiquing.
24. One-strokes may be splattered in various size dots.
25. One-stroke thinned 50-50 with water is used in airbrushes.
26. One-strokes may be used for designs on the banding wheel.
27. China painting techniques are possible with one-strokes.
28. Majolica-like effects are possible with one-stroke and glaze.
29. Mask may be used to cover design areas then remove to detail with one-stroke colors.
30. Wax-resist may be used as a mask and fired off for detail work.
31. One-strokes may be used over transparent glazes.
32. One-strokes may be used under transparent glazes.
33. One-stroke designs are possible over matte glazes.
34. One-strokes may be used only under transparent matte glaze.
35. One-strokes may be used to color embossing glazes as well as in combination techniques.
36. One-stroke designs are possible over froth and can be used to color it.
37. One-strokes are commonly used in design techniques over opaque underglazes.
38. One-strokes may be used in designs under crackle glazes.
39. Coloring ceramic slip is possible by adding one-stroke to it.
40. One-strokes are similar to printer's ink for printing and designs.
41. One-strokes may be used to tint lace slip.
42. One-strokes will tint porcelain to pastel colors.

GLOSSARY OF TERMS

AIRBRUSH: A spraying device used with compressed air to force paint into a fine mist. Used for shading or all over even coverage. Often used for special designs.

ANTIQUING: Washing down a piece to accentuate the detail.

BANDING WHEEL: A motorized or hand-driven turntable used to apply uniform bands of color on a piece or may be used to apply a varied, wavy pattern.

BISQUE: This is the name given to the clay body in ceramics once it has been fired. May also be called bisqueware.

BRISTLE: The element of brushes. This type of brush when so called is usually from the hair of the body of hogs and boars.

BROCADE: A decorating glaze used for raised or textured designs. May be used in combination with most other glazes.

BRUSHES: The means by which decorations are applied to ceramics. The type of work determines the type of brush.

CHINA PAINTING: The technique of applying paint to a piece. Usually done in fine detail and shading.

CLOUDING CLEAR OR TRANSPARENT GLAZES: Often caused by too heavy an application of glaze or not firing piece hot enough. Try refiring in a hotter kiln.

COATS: Usually recommended by the manufacturer; the number of layers of paint required.

CONE: More properly called pyrometric cone. Controls temperature of kiln.

CRACKLE GLAZES: Crackle glazes have been formulated to produce a pattern of cracks in the finished piece. To control the amount of cracking use a thin coat of glaze for a small pattern, a heavy coat for a large pattern. The bisque must be fired to an 06 to produce the proper base for this glaze.

CRAZING: Glaze appears to have tiny cracks in an irregular pattern.

DETAIL: The areas of design in our pieces that may be added on, or are parts of the original cast piece.

DIPPING: A special process of glazing pieces by dipping them into glaze rather than using a brush. Manufacturers have designed special glazes for this purpose.

FROTH: A glaze that leaves a foamy appearance when applied and fired. Commonly used to produce snow effect. Available in a variety of colors also.

GREENWARE: The term used to describe the molded clay body once it has been removed from the mold and before it is fired.

HIGH FIRE: Pieces fired in a kiln at maximum temperatures.

HIGHLIGHTS: Those lowered areas or crevices of design in pieces.

LACE: Used in porcelain and ceramic techniques by soaking in slip, applying and then firing out lace leaving the solid thin layer of clay. Must use cotton lace.

LACE DRAPING: The method of using cotton lace for skirts, etc.

LINER: Usually of sable quality, a long bristled brush for fine design work.

MATTE GLAZES: These glazes produce a smooth, dull finish. Care must be used in application since these glazes move very slightly and an even application is a necessity.

ONE-STROKES: Pure color pigment available in either translucent or opaque colors. Used for detail work on greenware and bisque.

OPAQUE: A solid color with a finish that you cannot see through.

OVERFIRING: When a kiln temperature goes beyond the desired degree and will often produce defects.

OVERGLAZE: Refers to that class of finishes that go over a glaze.

PALETTE: May be commercially made or simply a glazed tile that is used to mix colors on.

PATTERN: Basic outline of a design to follow in painting.

PEELING OF GLAZE: Usually found in the application of underglaze, it is caused by too heavy an application of glaze.

PINHOLES: A defect in glazes caused by underfiring bisque, applying glaze on greenware or firing too rapidly.

PORCELAIN: An extremely fine grade of high fire clay bodies. Sometimes called china clay.

RED SABLE: Term for brush hair which actually comes from the tail of the Kolinsky.

SATIN GLAZES: These glazes produce a smooth, soft color finish.

SEMI-MATTE GLAZES: These are basically the same as matte glazes but have a higher sheen.

SEMI-TRANSPARENT: Colors that have a see-through quality which varies depending on the colors underneath.

SGRAFFITO TOOL: Used for short stroke work and carving.

SILK SPONGE: A fine grained, pure sponge used in cleaning or design work.

SLIP: Clay suspended in water with chemicals.

SMOOTHED TEXTURED GLAZES: Can be caused by not applying enough of the glaze or overfiring.

SPATTERING: A painting technique of loading brush with paint and tapping brush with finger, dropping paint onto desired surface.

SPATULAS: Of plastic or metal, used for mixing paints.

SPONGE: Many varieties. Used for clean-up and decorating techniques.

SQUARE SHADER: A square shaped brush usually of sable quality.

STENCIL PAPER: Heavy, waxed, semi-transparent paper that keeps clear lines and is easily cut.

STENCILS: A cutout design in a specially waxed paper. Design is usually cut from several pieces of paper to allow application of varied colors in stages.

TECHNIQUES: Term used to denote the method of finishing a piece.

TEXTURED GLAZE: A glaze that is formulated to fire with a texture.

TRACING PAPER: Thin paper used to transfer designs to pieces.

TRANSLUCENT: Having the ability of allowing color or light to show through but in the process be diffused.

TRANSPARENT: Almost clear finish, slightly diffusing the colors beneath it.

TRANSPARENT GLAZES: Any glaze that you can see through to see the design or colors painted underneath.

TURNTABLE: A revolving table, usually round, that can be used to place pieces on during the decorating process.

UNDERFIRING: When the temperature of the kiln does not reach the proper degree. Will produce faults in finished pieces.

UNDERGLAZE: Paint used for all-over coverage on greenware. Approximately 60-80 percent clay in combination with color pigment. Three coats must be applied to attain proper color coverage. Because of the high clay content the color may be applied smoothly. Can be polished without glazing, or a clear or transparent glaze can be applied over to accent the color.

VISCOSITY: The ability of a fired piece to hold water without the application of a sealing glaze.

WAX RESIST: Used to mask portions of work where it is designed to show the color of the clay body in contrast to a colored background. Wax will burn out during the firing.

Potato Block Printing on Ceramics

By Dale Swant

Spuds are more than just staples of our diets. These inexpensive vegetables can be an art medium too. When cut in a variety of designs and used as printing blocks the results can be stimulating.

Potato printing is simple to do and would be a great project for kids too. You may print on almost anything including paper and ceramics. You can be as complex or as simple as you want. This is dependent only on how you carve your potatoes. Complicated patterns from one potato are possible and satisfactory, but using simple blocks in combination and printing several over each other usually produces the best results.

MATERIALS NEEDED

Several medium to large potatoes
Knife
One-Stroke Colors:
    Green
    Yellow
    Blue
    Red
    Brown
    Pink
    Black
Flat surface greenware
Clear Glaze
Glaze brush
Palette
Old Newspapers

USE NEW BLOCKS

Use new potato blocks each time you sit down to print. You will find that potatoes decompose easily and become soft when exposed to the air for a period of time. If you should happen to do your piece over several days you will need freshly cut, crisp potatoes to do the most effective job of printing.

Colors are determined by what you plan to print. Prints on paper can be achieved by using water base paints such as watercolors, tempra, etc. The papers you use matter little as long as they are absorbent. Ceramic greenware acts quite the same as paper and will absorb the colors nicely.

Keep in mind when purchasing colors that you can achieve excellent results by over-printing colors. Two colors printed in combination can produce a third. Red and yellow make orange, blue and yellow make green, etc.

Colors used here were Green, Yellow, Blue, Pink and several mixtures of these. The choice of one-strokes is up to you since flowers can be any color and still look nice.

To prepare your one-strokes for this printing use the same principles as if you were going to use a brush. The more water you add to your colors the lighter they will be. Normally we use one-strokes in a creamy consistency with a brush. To get the brightest colors when using potatoes mix them slightly thicker.

To load a potato with color use a brush and apply color to the face of your printing block. Stamp this block on paper to even the color. After doing this several times the color will work into the pores of the potato to give you more even coverage. Once you have the pores filled

Continued on page 28

you may use the potato like a rubber stamp and your color can be on a palette like a stamp pad. Apply color to your potato block and stamp once on paper to even color each time before applying to your greenware.

STEP-1—To begin, peel and clean several potatoes. If you have a definite design in mind you need to cut potato block stencils for each section and for each color of your design. For this project I cut two different size flower petals, a stem, center and leaf blocks.

Potatoes are grainy, thereby porous, and will absorb some of your one-stroke color. Therefore, if you plan on using several different colors of flowers as we are here, you will need separate masters for each flower petal color.

STEP-2—Clean greenware in the usual manner. Once cleaned, it is best to place your piece on a turntable so you may work from all sides without handling the piece.

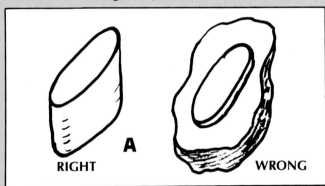

RIGHT   **A**   WRONG

CUTTING PRINTING BLOCKS

How you cut your blocks can add to the ease of printing on ceramics. Rather than cutting a potato in half, carving your design down from the surface slightly and printing with it, you should carve your design from the whole piece of the potato. (See Illustration A).

By doing this you can always tell which block is which and also enable yourself to see where you are printing as you do it. By cutting blocks incorrectly you are also running the danger of printing unwanted marks. It is easy to slop ink on the edge of a full potato and mistakenly put too much pressure on one side or the other when printing and mark your project in error. We do have the advantage of being able to remove mistakes from greenware with a damp sponge, but why not do it right in the first place.

With these basics you are now ready to attempt your first project. It is a good idea to experiment a few times before starting on a masterpiece. Cut some potatoes into triangles, circles, etc. and experiment with printing on paper. Then go on to your greenware project.

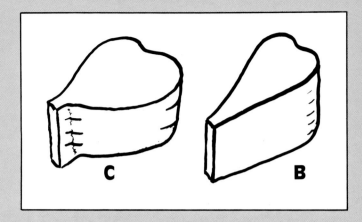

C   **B**

PRINTING FLOWERS

The project shown here was done using seven different potato block stencils.

The darker flowers were one shape (B) and the lighter flowers another (C). Because we are using more than one color here you will need one of (B) and two of (C). In addition the flowers with the petals shaped as in (C) were over-printed with a smaller petal the same shape (D).

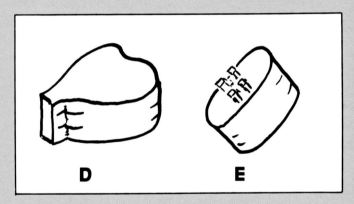

D   **E**

You need two different shaped blocks for leaves (F). One is a larger leaf that includes vein lines. The other is a streamer leaf (G) used as the bottom of the project. A straight line block was used for the stems (H).

The final block was for the center of the flowers (F).

Once you have your block stencils cut we are ready to print.

Colors used here were Green, Yellow, Blue, Pink and several mixtures of these. The choice of colors is up to you since flowers can be any color and still look nice.

STEP-3—To start printing you use lightest colors first. There are two Yellow, Blue-Purple and Pink flowers. Start by printing your Yellow flowers then the Blue-Purple. The arrangement is up to you. The only thing to remember is to allow enough room between, but print them close enough to each other so that when printing the other flowers later, you allow a little

Continued on page 29

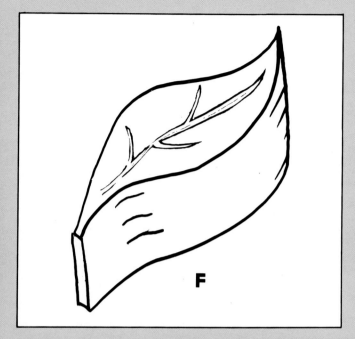

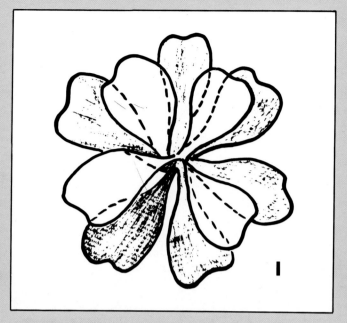

overlap. Cover the colors beneath the overlap to give your piece a three dimensional look.

When printing your Blue-Purple flowers, print the Blue petals first then go back over your flowers with alternate petals of Purple. (I). This gives you a flower with three color tones.

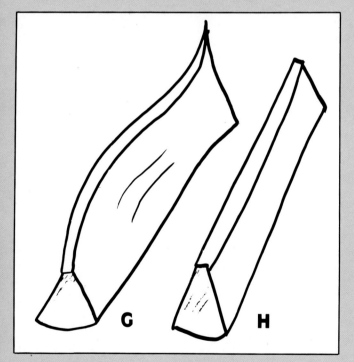

STEP-4—Next, using block (H) print your stems. Since you cannot make a stem block as long as a full stem, you have to use this block and print it end to end several times to get long stems.

STEP-5—Print your leaves using blocks (F) and (G). Place them so they look natural to you.

STEP-6—Final step is to take block (E) in hand and print the centers of your flowers.

Be sure each color of one-stroke is dry before you overprint any additional colors.

STEP-7—When you have your piece printed to your satisfaction take your black or dark brown one-stroke and apply outlines to your flower petals with a fine brush. You may also wish to stroke in the centers of the flowers using alternate strokes of Yellow and Brown.

STEP-8—When all colors are dry fire piece to 04-05, glaze with Clear or Transparent glaze and refire to 05-06.

You will find potato block printing rewarding and a lot of fun. Use your imagination on what types of items to print.

Keep in mind that on any project you plan that takes a long time and laps into another day, that you will need fresh blocks the second day if you want to complete the job properly. If you don't want to recarve, you best complete projects at one sitting.

Now Have Fun!. . .

Guest Artists....

No book on one-strokes would be complete without some examples of how to use this versatile ceramic decorating media. On the following pages we have included several examples of work decorated in one-strokes by different artists. Each writer is nationally known for their ceramic decorating ability. These artists are kind enough to share their ideas with students all over the world and we are fortunate to be able to include their ideas here.

Featured artists are:
Sande Scoredos
David Hoff
Diane Murphree
Natalie Kahn
Leila Sloan
Larry Rhodes

Pinecones on Porcelain

By Sande Scoredos

Pinecones are truly one of nature's winter beauties. The formation of the pinecones makes a perfect shading project for us. The brush-strokes used can easily be accomplished with a little practice. Proper shading is the key to shadows and highlights, letting the brush do all of the work.

The candle has been added for extra flair and the design as a whole will contribute to an elegant holiday setting.

MATERIALS NEEDED

Suitable porcelain greenware
Underglazes:
  Tan
  Light Green
  Light Yellow
One-Strokes:
  Dark Green
  Dark Yellow
  Red Brown
  Black
  White
Red China paint
Liquid Bright Gold
Airbrush
Wax resist
Clear Gloss Glaze
Brushes:
  #1 Scripto
  #6 and 8 Shaders
  #5 Round
Tracing paper
Clay carbon
Cleaning tool
Sponge
Glazed tile

STEP-1—Fettle ware carefully. Extra care should be exercised when cleaning porcelain. Fire piece to cone 05.

STEP-2—Apply wax resist to lip rim and lid where pieces touch. Apply Clear glaze to inside of jar and lid, wiping off any excess that gets on wax resist.

STEP-3—Trace design onto tracing paper and transfer main outline of design only to piece at this time, no details.

STEP-4—Block in candle and leaves with two coats of Light Green underglaze, pinecones with two coats of Tan and flame with two coats of Light Yellow.

STEP-5—Align traced pattern onto piece, slide clay carbon under tracing paper and transfer detail of design. Trace pinecone and candle detail exactly.

STEP-6—Practice the following side-loading and shading procedure with a flat shader before you begin on the piece itself. First, rinse brush in water. Using a damp sponge, pat brush on sponge to remove excess water and to flatten and chisel the shader. Pick up a little color on one side of brush, begin

Continued on page 32

carefully to keep color on one-quarter of brush only. Now, place brush down flat on a glazed tile and make a flat stroke to blend color, always blending on a clean area of tile. This will flatten the brush. Check for proper loading and blend color from a deep shade, fading into clear water. All four of these steps are very important: rinse, pat, side-load, blend. Don't skip any of them. Now that you have practiced this procedure, you are ready to shade.

STEP-7—Side-load shader with Dark Green and shade candle and leaves. Deepen shadowed areas with Black shading. Shade flame and halo with Dark Yellow, and the pinecones with Red Brown. The shader is placed with the color shading behind each layer, using a slightly wiggled stroke.

STEP-8—Turn brush over and shade each turnback individually. Shade lightly with Black between the two pinecones to separate and create a shadow.

STEP-9—Using a scripto brush, stroke in pine needles with Light and Dark Greens.

STEP-10—Mix Black and Red Brown and detail the entire pattern. Add lots of fine lines to pinecones and detail the turnbacks. Add White highlights to turnbacks.

STEP-11—Airbrush the edges with Dark Green.

STEP-12—Fire piece to cone 6.

STEP-13—Apply Red china paint to berries and Firing Gold to tendrils and rim of lid. Detail flowers with Gold.

STEP-14—Fire piece to cone 018.

Magnolia and Hibiscus

By David Hoff

We are extremely lucky to have a wide variety of colors, medias and designs to work with these days. Years ago, powdered glazes and a few underglazes were enough to give pleasure in our chosen hobby, but they were limiting. Now, vast choices on how to finish a piece are available to almost every hobbyist and studio owner in most every town. Therefore, when I discovered the Magnolia and Hibiscus in a Florida studio, I knew I wanted to share this multi-media project with you.

We will be using a combination of translucent underglaze colors, an airbrush, both gloss and matte finish clear glazes and a black matte glaze to achieve a very natural delicate quality. I suggest that you take your time with this project, and while you are working on it, think about other flowers and how you would complete them.

We will be working on both flowers throughout, so let's get started.

MATERIALS NEEDED
Magnolia and Hibiscus greenware
One-strokes:
  Rose
  Cinderella Pink
  Irish Green
  Mahogany Brown
  French Brown
  Sienna Brown
  Cobalt Jet Black
  White
  Grass Green

  Chartreuse
  Mulberry
  Yellow Orange
  Leaf Green
Glazes:
  Clear brushing
  Stardust Matte
  Really Black
  Patch-A-Tach
3/4'' Glaze brush
Airbrush with #5 tips
Cleanup tool
Silk sponge
Turntable
Palette knife
Greenware mender
Glue
  STEP-1—Carefully clean your greenware. Keep all of the parts to the flowers separated, as it will be both easier to clean and decorate if parts are not attached. Sponge entire working area lightly. Be careful not to damage

Continued on page 34

detail or to break magnolia petals.

STEP-2—Prepare your work area. Set up the airbrush with an H-3 tip (medium size). Set out several three ounce plastic airbrush bottles, bowl of clean water, 3/4" glaze brush, turntable and palette knife, greenware mending material and one-stroke colors. Also set out the parts to each flower.

STEP-3—Using a mixture of four parts water to one part color, pre-thin all of your one-stroke colors. Mix one-stroke color with water and mix vigorously with your glaze brush to eliminate the need for straining your product. With your air pressure regulated to 40 pounds PSI and your airbrush nozzle open two revolutions, spray Magnolia blossoms with White. Be sure to cover both sides of the blossom.

STEP-4—Add a very small amount of pre-thined Irish Green one-stroke to the White. Add enough color to give you a "mint" green look. Delicately begin to shade the center area of both sections of your magnolia. Continue building color until the green on your flower matches the green in your jar. Note: when the color in the jar and the color applied to piece match, you have applied enough color to prevent fade out during the glaze fire.

STEP-5—Next, add some Sienna Brown to the remaining mixture of "Mint" green to form a greenish brown mixture. Again, spray into the center area of both parts of your magnolia. This time also spray your center section of the Magnolia blossom. Tips of Magnolia blossom should be kept the whitest. Next, apply this mixture to the top side of your hibiscus flower. A light application will

be enough. Remember to keep six inches away from the ware while airbrushing the color.

STEP-6—Clean out your airbrush bottles and then spray Chartreuse one-stroke over both sets of leaves, both front and back. Lightly spray Chartreuse on the large section of the magnolia blossom's under side. This will enhance the reflective qualities of flower and leaves.

STEP-7—Add Leaf Green to the Chartreuse and shade the back sides of both sets of leaves. The backside of both the magnolia and the hibiscus leaves are much lighter than their top sides. When applying color, angle your airbrush in such a way that the color works its way from the tip of each leaf to the base. The color will literally flow along the edge of each leaf. Once the back side of each leaf has been finished, turn your magnolia leaves over and spray the top side of these leaves. Shade the top side as you did the back side and repeat with hibiscus leaf. Work from tip of each leaf to its base.

STEP-8—Add Grass Green to this mixture and gently cross shade the back side of both sets of leaves. To cross shade, angle your airbrush so that color crosses the ware at an almost horizontal plane to the greenware. The color will stay mainly in the crease of the leaves. Turn both sets of leaves over and give the top sides a generous application of the Grass Green mixture.

Again, use your cross shading angle. The magnolia leaves should be a bit darker than the hibiscus. Apply Grass Green mixture slowly and let the color build up to suit your liking. Before washing the green out, highlight your branch with bits of Grass Green here and there like moss growing on a branch.

STEP-9—Apply one even coat

of Cinderella Pink to both sides of the hibiscus. The previously applied color mixture done in **Step-5** will show through the pink after the glaze firing.

STEP-10—Airbrush the center and the edges of the hibiscus with Rose and airbrush color on outside edges of hibiscus flower, top and bottom.

STEP-11—Repeat **Step-10,** first, adding Mulberry to the Rose one-stroke. Also apply a bit of this mixture to your hibiscus leaves. Just a light misting to enhance your piece.

STEP-12—Spray the Mulberry mixture on your hibiscus stamens.

STEP-13—Airbrush a generous coat of Mahogany onto the branch. Then darken with French Brown and shade underside of Magnolia leaves and shade your branch. Spray hibiscus calix with both browns and a bit of Cobalt Jet Black.

STEP-14—Assemble and attach your blossom parts as follows, using water and mending material. Secure pistal to center of the magnolia, then the center section to the large magnolia petal. Attach pistal to center of hibiscus. Make sure you cannot see greenware mender after attaching parts.

STEP-15—Fire to cone 03/04.

STEP-16—Mix one-third part water with two-thirds Stardust matte glaze. Using a #5 airbrush tip, apply three thin coats of glaze to all parts of flowers and leaves of Magnolia leaves.

The top sides of the magnolia leaves are airbrushed with clear gloss. Mix the clear glaze one third water to two thirds glaze and also apply three coats.

STEP-17—Apply Really Black glaze with your 3/4" glaze brush to round base.

STEP-18—Stilt and fire all pieces to a cone 05.

STEP-19—Glue all remaining parts of the flowers, using photograph for guide and enjoy.

Pretty Pansies

By Diane Murphree

With this pattern you can add more pansies by taking part of the pattern and tracing off more if wished. Add a small butterfly or rearrange as you wish.

STEP-1—Trace pattern onto greenware piece using clay-trace paper. Greenware should be dry. If you wish a background, mask off whole design. Let dry. Put Chartreuse out on palette, thin to a cream consistency. Use an almost dry silk sponge and pounce in background, more solidly near design and gradually feather out to one-half inch beyond design. Dry one half-hour. While waiting, put out Light Green, Dark Green, and a Blue Green on palette. Thin Light Green like milk, others like cream. Put out a bit of Red and some Black Green or Dark Green mixed with a tiny bit of Black. Remove mask by rubbing off with finger tips.

STEP-2—Using a #8 flat sable shader loaded in Light Green, side dip in Dark Green and then tip same side in Blue Green, stroke in all sepals, seed pod and stems, keeping Blue Green to edges. Use same brush, load same way and stroke in leaves, stroke in from each scallop tip to center vein, use two strokes keeping Blue Green to veins. Now stroke down a few tips of Red, mostly near tips of leaves. Use a detail brush and outline leaves going down each vein as you do this, put in the center vein, in the Black Green and also outline sepals and stems with same. Clean off palette.

STEP-3—Put out a quantity of Light Blue, Medium Blue, Dark Blue, Lilac or Orchid, Dark Purple, Red Brown, Black Brown or mix a tiny bit of Black into Red

Continued on page 36

—35—

Brown, Yellow, Orange and Camel's Tan or Taupe, and a bit of Black. Make all like cream. Add a bit of White, very thin. The following numbered flowers correspond to those on the pattern.

1. Top Pansy: Use a #10 flat shader (sable). Load in Lilac or Orchid, side well in Dark Purple. Stroke in two top petals, keeping Purple to edges. Stroke from bottom up and around all the way on larger petal. If center is not filled use Lilac or Orchid and stroke up to fill, fanwise.

Load brush in Light Blue, side dip well in Medium Blue, tip same side in two side petals, keeping Purple to edges. Now stroke in bottom center petal same way. If center is White stroke in with Light Blue from centers to edge.

2. Half Open Pansy at Top: Load brush with White, side dip in Light Blue, tip same side in Lilac or Orchid and stroke in top and bottom petals first and center petals last. Keep Lilac or Orchid to edges. Leave White, if any, in center of petals. Stroke very lightly up from base fanwise a bit of Yellow about 3/8 inch.

3. Pansy in Center: Load brush in Red Brown. Side dip in Black Brown. Process same as top pansy's upper petals. Load brush in Yellow, side dip well in Orange, tip same side in Camel Tan or Taupe and process other three petals, same as first pansy.

4. Bottom Pansy below one just done: Load brush in Medium Blue, side dip in Dark Blue and process same as first pansy's upper petals. Load brush in Light Blue, side dip in Medium Blue, stroke in three bottom petals as you did others.

For Another Pansy: If you put one in, all petals are same loading but be sure to work from top petals down to bottom petals. Load brush in Yellow,

**ORIGINAL DESIGN
BY
DIANE MURPHREE**

side dip very well in Orange and keep Orange to edges. Buds would be best done in the blues and Lilac or Orchid. Stroke with swirl lines.

STEP-4—Using a #4 pointed round brush, outline petals on top pansy with darkest blue. On all flowers use this outlining by thin lines but press and make heavy as you do inward curves or scallops.

On red brown petals of center pansy use Black. On its lower petals use Red Brown. On blue pansy use Dark Blue on upper petals, Medium Blue on lower petals. On half open flower and buds, use Lilac or Orchid. On yellow pansy use Camel's Tan or Taupe. Now on all pansies, stroke in a little ways some fine lines where shown on pattern

Continued on page 39

Classic Vase

By Natalie Kahn

Create a modern day classic by combining molds that together produce an original ceramic composition. The pitcher, with realistically detailed figures and designs from mythology, and the graceful pedestal make an appealing vase or decorative accent that will blend with many interior settings. A translucent underglaze dramatizes the interesting detailing and harmonizes perfectly with the richly tinted Gloss Glaze used for the final finish. Place it in your home and add some of the ornate beauty of Victorian times plus the warmth of color that is so popular today!

MATERIALS NEEDED

Greenware compote
 Cherub base
Accessories bowl
Short lid without knob only
Decorative Pitcher
Greenware wet
Translucent Underglaze
 French Brown
Gloss Glaze
 Golden Honey
Brushes:
 Liner
 Glaze
Small pointed knife
Cleanup tool
Slip
Glazed tile

STEP-1—While greenware is wet, use small pointed knife to cut away handle and base of pitcher. Also trim away upper lip and portion of pitcher along edges of raised designs. Cut away inside rim of lid. Use cleanup tool to score bottom edge of lid, bottom of vase and top of base. Working with one piece at a time, apply slip to scratched areas and attach vase to inverted lid and base to center of lid by gently pressing pieces together.

STEP-2—Prepare greenware.

STEP-3—Mix ¼ teaspoon French Brown with ½ teaspoon water on glazed tile. Use liner brush to shade all raised details with thinned color.

STEP-4—Next, use ¼ teaspoon French Brown with ¼ teaspoon water on glazed tile. Use liner brush to outline and detail all raised designs with thinned color.

STEP-5—Bisque fire to cone 05.

STEP-6—Make sure piece is free of dust. Use glaze brush to apply 3 even coats Golden Honey completely over piece.

STEP-7—Glaze fire to cone 06.

Polychrome Effect in One-Stroke

By Leila Sloan

Delft Blue and Polychrome Delft are the best known forms of Delft. Polychrome is similar to Majolica, Fience, and Persian Kubatcha Ware. The latter may have been responsible for all other related forms as this is the granddaddy of them all, so to speak.

There are many ways of obtaining like results, even though the processes seem to be unrelated. I think this is what makes ceramics such a fascinating field to study and research.

Many Colors

The prefex "poly" means many and "chrome" means color. We have a much wider range of color, therefore, than in the conventional Delft, which must confine itself to the three shades of one color.

Glazes, enamels, one-strokes, velvets, underglazes or china paints may be the medium, giving a wide choice.

The flowers may be yellow, orange or red-orange for the lightest shades, accented with the dark reds and purples, with blue and green for the leaves and possibly an olive green for the grassy and fernlike areas.

For detail you may choose from the following: dark brown, dark blue or green, purple, maroon or black. After firing to cone 05 to set the color, glaze with the blue gray tinted transparent glaze.

Tinting Glaze

The tinting of the glaze is done by taking some of the one-stroke color, thinning it very much, mix-ing it into a uniform mixture and then adding it to the transparent glaze, being sure to thoroughly mix the two together.

Test firings are most important to determine whether the shade is correct and the mixture complete so that there is no streaking. As for the shade it may be definite or subtle however you like it.

MATERIALS NEEDED
Bisqueware
One-Stroke Colors:
   Yellow
   Orange
   Red
   Purple
   Blue
   Green
   Black
   Brown
Clear Glaze
Tile

Continued on page 39

Palette Knife
Pencil
Pattern
Brushes:
  #6, 8 or 10 Goldina
    or Red Round Sable Brushes
  #4 or larger liner or
    Scripto brush
Water
One-stroke media
Sponge

STEP-1—Carefully clean the greenware and fire to cone 05. It is preferable to work on bisque with one-stroke because (1) your color shows to greater advantage when completed, (2) the consistency of the one-stroke does not have to be as exact as it does on greenware and may be more representative of the individual without all the possible mishaps that might occur if you are working on greenware.

The larger flowers are your lightest colors, the smaller are your darker. Accent any areas of flowers with a darker color than that used on the flower itself. Yellow, Orange, Red and Purple are flower and blossom colors.

STEP-2—Leaves are done in Blue and Green and the smaller graduated fern-like leaves which typlify Polychrome may be one part of Green to two parts of Orange, giving an Olive-Green color.

All flowers and leaves are painted from outermost points toward center or stems. When applying color, great care is taken to allow white edges on sides of petals and tips so that they are distinguishable one from the other in layer on layer or overlapping.

When detail is done, very fine, even lines are used around petals (allowing the white to remain inside the detail thus becoming part of your flower), in contrast to heavier lines around leaves (no white will remain here) and for stems.

STEP-3—I usually detail in Black but in Polychrome you have a wide choice of Blue, Green, Black, Brown, Purple, or Magenta. Any of the colors should have Black added to them to noticeably darken them from the areas where they have been used in the design.

STEP-4—Centers of flowers are done in the darkest or detail color. Two coats are applied and an area is allowed to remain White, creating a highlight.

For large, solid areas the consistency must be very thin, almost like water. Five to seven coats are applied, allowing the water from the previous coat to bind the area to the color being painted until a substantial buildup has been created to give an all-over effect.

Possibly the best way to determine the number of coats necessary would be through your own knowledge of handling of glaze. If you tend to be a heavy glazer, five coats would be sufficient; if you are a normal glazer six coats would do; if you are a light glazer, seven or possibly eight coats would be required.

STEP-5—After painting, fire to cone 05 to set one-stroke.

STEP-6—Clear glaze is used as a base tinted with very thin mixture of one-stroke with water, using any of the colors used in the Polychrome. For example, your glaze may be tinted into a very pale Yellow, Orange, Red, Blue, Green or Purple. It is advisable that before glazing, a test be made to determine (1) whether the shade satisfies and (2) whether or not the mixture is complete so as not to cause streaking. Apply three coats of glaze, fire and behold!

Is there any doubt as to why the Polychrome has endured through the ages as one of the many outstanding forms of Delft?

using color you used on outlining petals. Put Yellow in where tent shape is in center of pansies, outline finely in Black and put a tiny dot of green in center of them. Use Red Brown for other detail, fan shapes on yellow and brown pansies, Purple on others, then a bit of Black fanning out over that, very fine lines.

STEP-5—Now sgraffito fine highlights fanwise on lower petals, about center of petal or 1/4-inch from edges, just to give highlights. Sgraffito out a tiny solid fan shape at bottom of tent part on petal and fill with Yellow. Sgraffito deeply a curved "fingernail appearing shape" to each side of tent center. Curve inward and let tips touch at top, thus. Sgraffito highlights, about 3/8 inch from tips down each leaf section towards center vein and a fine line on stems and each sepal point and seed pod.

STEP-6—Fire at cone 05. Glaze with a satin matte transparant glaze. Where so much sgraffito is done, always put a primer coat, so to say, of the glaze as thin as water, working in well where sgraffito lines are, then glaze as label says. This makes sure no air will lay in sgraffito parts. Fire again at cone 06.

Frostina, The Snow Woman

By Larry Rhodes

In this era of Women's Liberation, I guess it's about time for a little equal representation on the snow scene. But you'll notice I haven't given up my traditions completely... Frostina is still carrying a broom. Well, ladies, maybe she only uses it on the occasional chauvinist passing by. In any case, during the holiday season, may your days be bright!

MATERIALS NEEDED

Greenware plate, 10″
Maxi bander
Wax resist
Brushes:
  ®6 Goldina
  ®10 Square Shader
  ®1 Scripto
  1″ Flat Glaze
  ¼″ Dry Flat
One-Strokes:
  Turquoise Blue
  Red Brown
  Winter White
  Jet Black
  Camel Tan
  Yellow
  Dark Green
  Chocolate Brown
Underglazes:
  Ice Green
  Forest Green
  Flesh
Lead-Free Glazes:
  Clear Glare
  Poppy

STEP-1—Clean the ware carefully. Trace on pattern.

STEP-2—Using a maxi bander, measure a border of about one-half inch all around the plate.

STEP-3—Cover the figure of the snow lady completely with White one-stroke. Use three coats of coverage of Flesh one-stroke on the hat, broom and handle.

STEP-4—Apply three coats of Ice Green underglaze to the holly leaves on the border and the one in the lady's hat.

STEP-5—Use the ¼″ dry flat brush to drybrush Yellow and Tan one-strokes on the broom bristles. Corner load a #10 square shader and apply Red Brown one-stroke to the hat, broom and handle.

STEP-6—Shade the snow under milady's feet with Turquoise Blue, corner loaded on the #10 square shader and drybrushed. Corner load the square shader with Dark Green one-stroke and shade all the holly.

STEP-7—Block in the stripes on the scarf with Forest Green underglaze, referring to photo for placement.

STEP-8—Use Chocolate Brown one-stroke to color the hat band and shadow under the hat.

STEP-9—Detail the piece using a #2 scripto with Black one-stroke. The lettering is optional and is done with Dark Green one-stroke.

STEP-10—Bisque fire to cone 04-05, preferably 04.

STEP-11—Apply one coat of wax resist wherever you want the red to appear on your piece, the stripes, berries and border. Brush on three thin coats of lead-free Clear glaze. Make sure when working with lead-free glazes that you brush them out as smoothly as possible. Do not allow the coats to overlap, leaving ridges to build up.

STEP-12—Fire to cone 05. Lead-free glazes should always be fired to 05 to mature properly. Underfiring may result in roughness, non-clarity, color variations and sometimes a texturing of the clay.

STEP-13—Now apply a lead-free Poppy. Puddle on three coats of this glaze to the stripes and berries. Brush on four coats of Poppy to the back of the plate and on your pre-measured border. Remember to follow the suggestions for applying lead-free glazes, brushing as smoothly as possible. Remove any Poppy that may have gotten on the Clear Glare glazed areas.

STEP-14—Refire to cone 05.